A VISIT TO THE BAHAMAS from A to Z

MW01137246

KNOWLEDGE is CAPITAL
PUBLISHING & EDUCATIONAL PROGRAMS

www.knowledgeiscapital.com

First Edition

© 2020 Veronica McFall. All rights reserved.

No part of this publication may be reproduced, stored in a retrieval system
or transmitted in any form by any means electronic, mechanical, or photocopying,
recording or otherwise without the permission of the author or Knowledge is Capital,
Incorporated.

For more information please contact:
Knowledge is Capital
knowledgeiscapital1@gmail.com

ISBN 978-0-578-30257-7 (softcover)
ISBN 978-0-578-99532-8 (eBook)

A VISIT TO THE BAHAMAS from A to Z

Dedication

George Sr. and Evangeline - my parents and first teachers who encouraged me to explore the world.

George Jr. and Kathleen - my first travel buddies who remember all the great trips we experienced with mom and dad.

Vanessa, Evan, and Andrew - keep learning and traveling the world.

Maurice - thanks for the adventure of a lifetime.

Children of The Bahamas and the world - the future depends upon you.

Acknowledgements:

The author wishes to express her deepest gratitude to those who were instrumental in the development and production of this project:

RJ Jenkins - thank you for making a childhood dream come true.
Vanessa Willoughby
Patrick Doyle
Brian M. Rowland
Robert Powley
Mrs. Rosamund & Mr. Ambrose DaCosta Williams and family
Mrs. Christine & Mr. Harcourt Rolle and family
Descendants of Clan McFall, Hanna, Heastie, Tynes of Acklins, Bahamas
Descendants of Clan Johnson of Eleuthera, Bahamas
Dr. Gail Saunders
Dr. James & Mrs. Bernadette Moultrie
Dr. Davidson Hepburn
Charles De Meola
Felicia Halpert
The National Archives of The Bahamas
The New York Public Library- Schomburg Center for Research in Black Culture.
The Gottesman Library, Teachers College, Columbia University
Butler Library, Columbia University
Glen Rock Public Library, Glen Rock, NJ

-VM

Dedication

Anne Marie - thank you for your unconditional love, encouragement and support of me during this project. I appreciate you more than you can know.

Rose and Jonah - thank you both for who you are now and who you are becoming.
Your childhood has been an amazing adventure I have been blessed to share with you.
As you grow up, keep learning and pursue the things that inspire you.

Melody and Brian - mom and dad, thank you for encouraging the artist in me from a young age. Your support has been unwavering and unending.

Josh - thank you for sharing a childhood full of creativity and fun with me. The adventures of the two brothers in this book have reinforced how important our brotherhood is to me.

Mary Dyer, my teacher - thank you for helping to instill in me the confidence I needed to pursue art further. It is one of the best decisions I've ever made.

Acknowledgements:

The illustrator wishes to express his sincere gratitude to Veronica McFall for her collaboration, trust, support and friendship during the making of this book. This experience has been a wonderful journey of discovery!

-RJ

KNOWLEDGE is CAPITAL
PUBLISHING & EDUCATIONAL PROGRAMS

www.knowledgeiscapital.com
First Edition
© Veronica McFall. All rights reserved.

No part of this publication may be reproduced, stored in a retrieval system or transmitted in any form by any means electronic, mechanical, or photocopying, recording or otherwise without the permission of the author or Knowledge is Capital, Incorporated.

All rights, including trademark rights, in and to the Olympic Symbol (5-Rings), along with the marks Olympian, Olympic(s) and Olympic Games are owned by the International Olympic Committee (IOC), and are owned and/or controlled in the United States by the U.S. Olympic and Paralympic Committee (USOPC). Reference to or use of such marks in this publication is not intended to imply any affiliation with or endorsement by the IOC or USOPC.

For more information please contact:
Knowledge is Capital
knowledgeiscapital1@gmail.com

ISBN 978-0-578-30257-7 (softcover)
ISBN 978-0-578-99532-8 (eBook)

A VISIT TO THE BAHAMAS from A to Z

WRITTEN BY
VERONICA MCFALL

ILLUSTRATED BY
RJ JENKINS

PUBLISHED BY
KNOWLEDGE IS CAPITAL

with **DATO THE FACT CAT AND THE VOYAGERS**

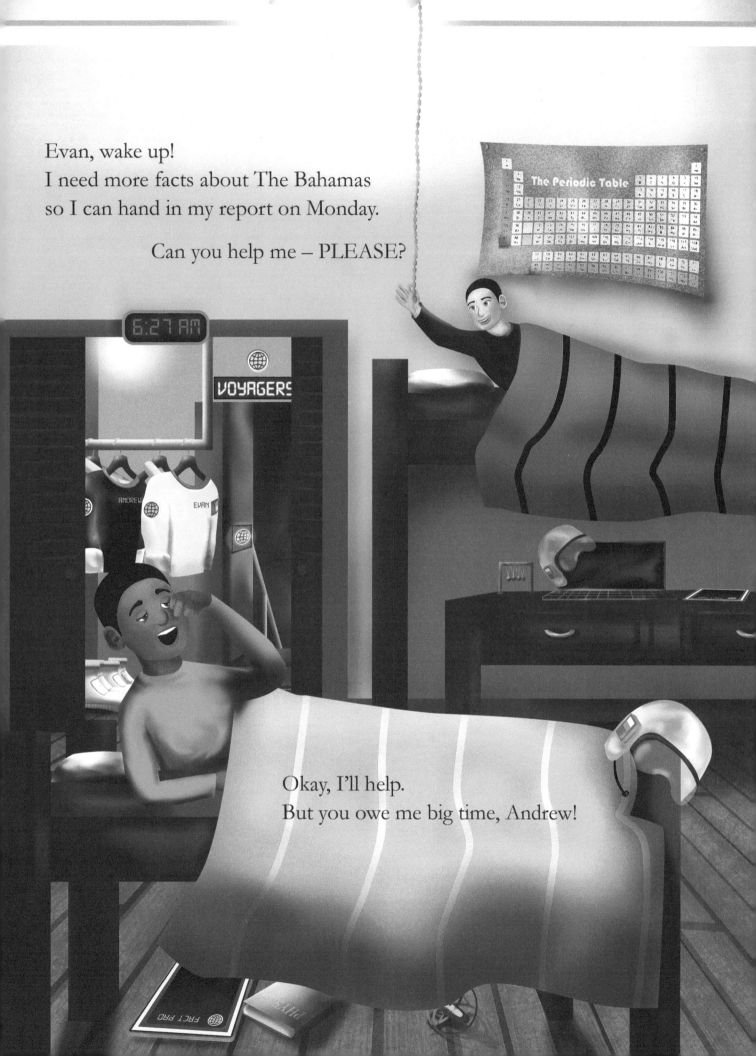

Evan, wake up!
I need more facts about The Bahamas
so I can hand in my report on Monday.

Can you help me – PLEASE?

Okay, I'll help.
But you owe me big time, Andrew!

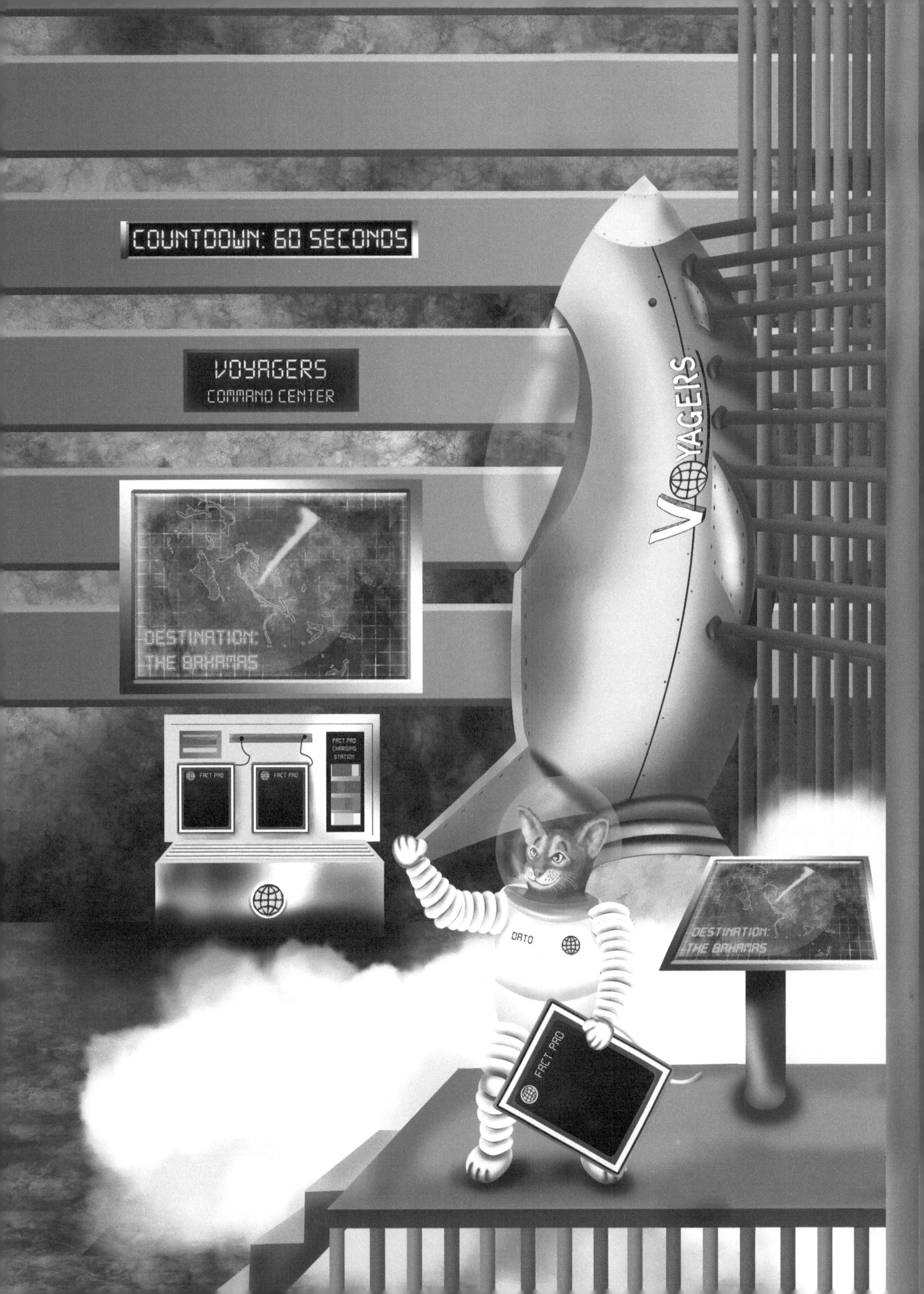
COUNTDOWN: 60 SECONDS
VOYAGERS
COMMAND CENTER
DESTINATION:
THE BAHAMAS
VOYAGERS
FACT PAD
FACT PAD
FACT PAD
CHARGING
STATION
DATO
FACT PAD
DESTINATION:
THE BAHAMAS

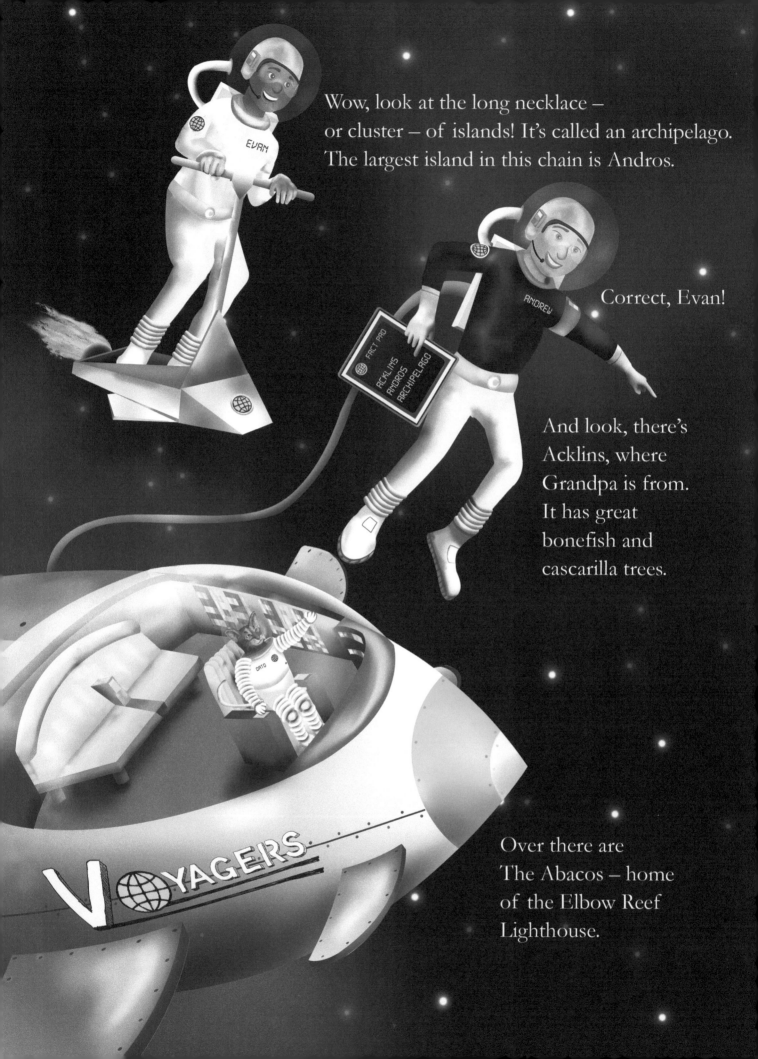

Now let's go meet
cousin Vanessa!

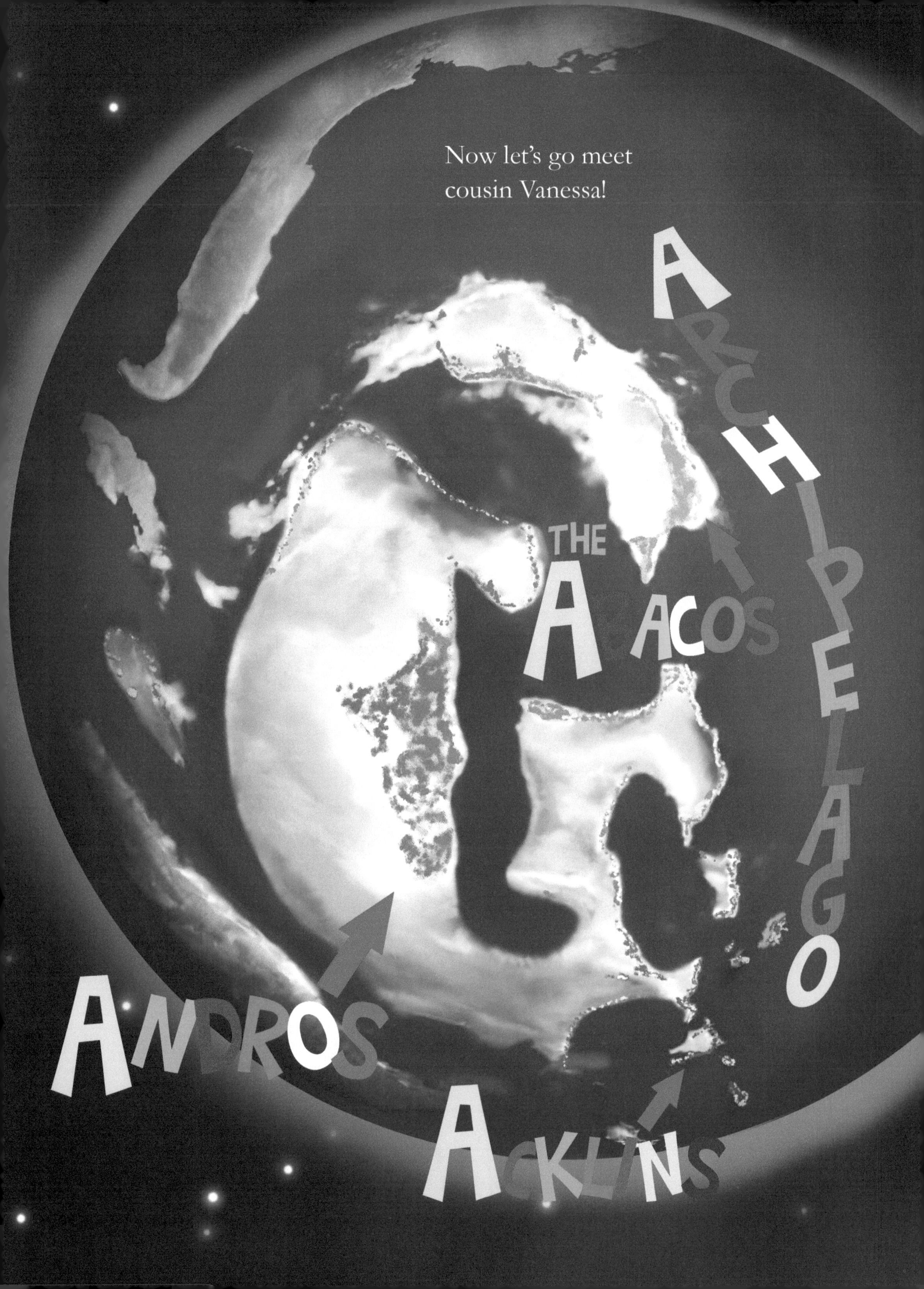

THE

ARCHIPELAGO

ABACOS

ANDROS

ACKLINS

Welcome, to The Bahamas,
Dato, Evan, and Andrew!

Since you just flew over the archipelago,
let's move on to the letter B.

Fact pads
ready?

On your mark,
get set, go!

The Bahamas got its name from two Spanish words:
baja - which means "low"; and *mar* — which means "sea."

THE
BAHAMAS

Grand
Bahama
The
Abacos
Bimini
Berry
Islands
Spanish
Wells
Harbor
Island
New
Providence
Eleuthera
Andros
Cat
Island
San
Salvador
The
Exumas
Rum
Cay
Long Island
Ragged
Island
Crooked
Island
Mayaguana
Acklins
Little
Inagua
Great
Inagua

So, *Baja Mar* means land of the shallow sea.
The Bahamas is a country of 700 islands,
and 2,400 cays. Bahamians live on just 30
of the islands.

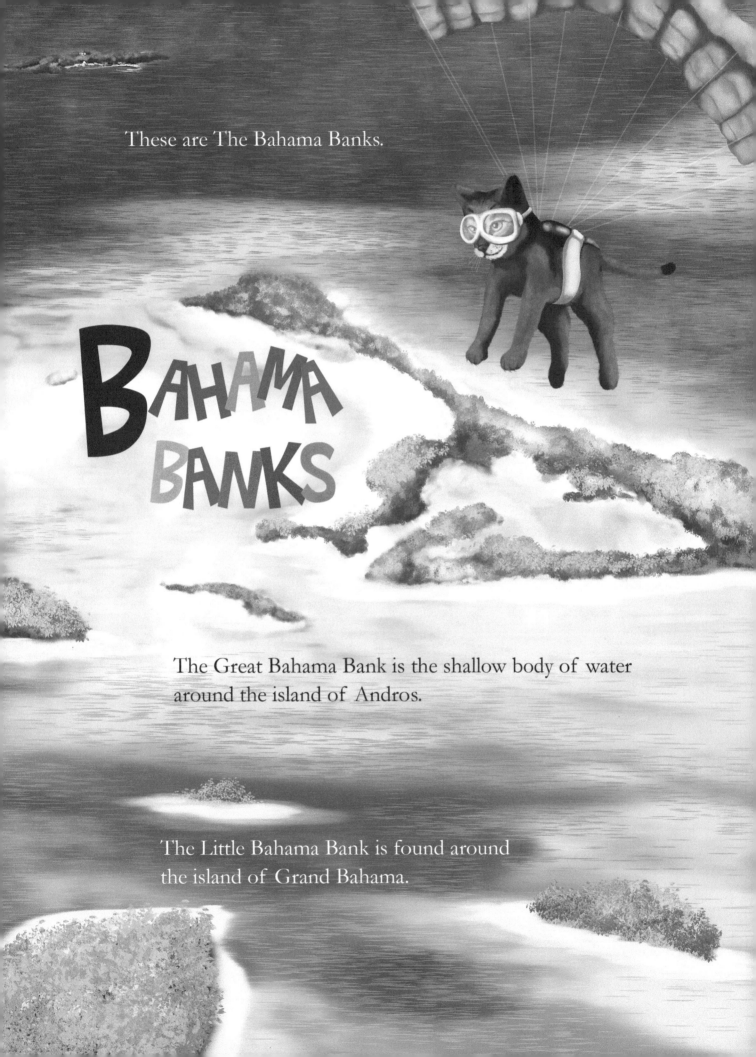

These are The Bahama Banks.

BAHAMA BANKS

The Great Bahama Bank is the shallow body of water around the island of Andros.

The Little Bahama Bank is found around the island of Grand Bahama.

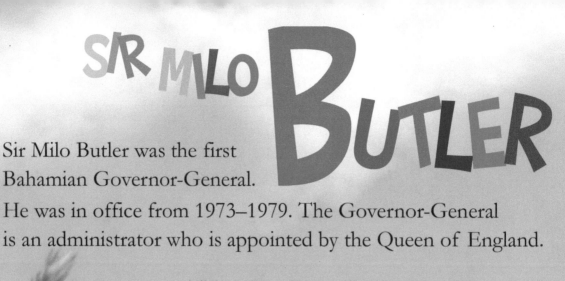

SIR MILO BUTLER

Sir Milo Butler was the first
Bahamian Governor-General.
He was in office from 1973–1979. The Governor-General
is an administrator who is appointed by the Queen of England.

This bust of Sir Milo was created
by the Bahamian sculptor,
Randolph W. Johnson.
It's located on the island
of New Providence, in Rawson Square.

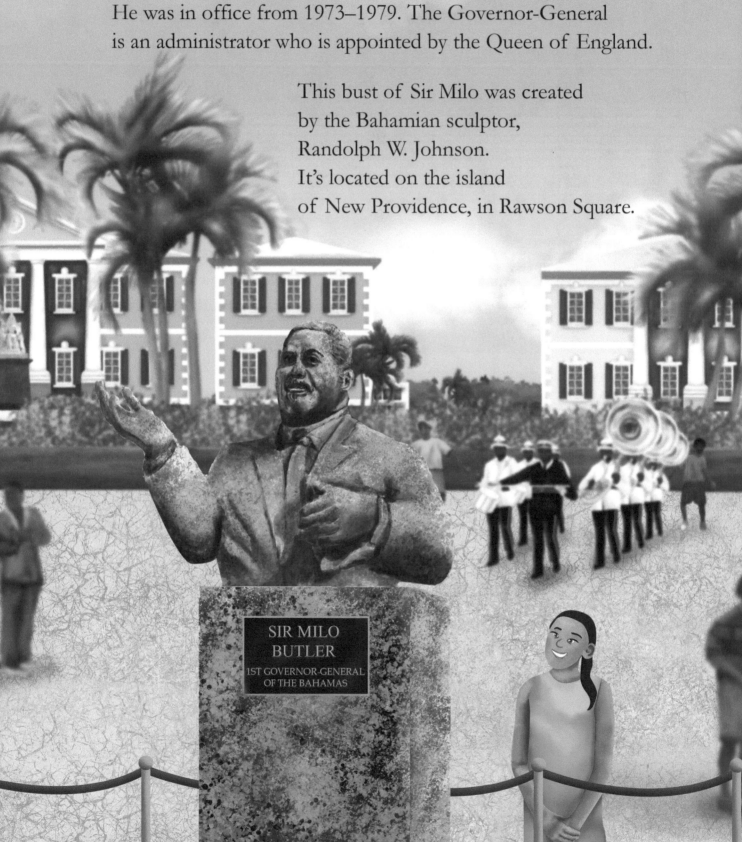

SIR MILO
BUTLER
1ST GOVERNOR-GENERAL
OF THE BAHAMAS

The beautiful Bahama Parrot eats guavas, berries, and seeds. It is about 12–13 inches long.

BAHAMA PARROT

CONCH

The conch lives inside of the beautiful conch shell and travels along the ocean floor. The foot has a claw-like end.

Conch is a very popular food in The Bahamas.
Even so, efforts are being made to conserve the conch
to prevent extinction.

CAY

A small, low, sandy island located on the edge of a coral reef is called a cay.

 FACT PAD

MOST CAYS IN
THE BAHAMAS
ARE UNINHABITED—
NO ONE LIVES
ON THEM

Coral is made up of lots and lots
of tiny living creatures called polyps.

Coral grows underwater and is very colorful.
It hardens as it grows and can develop into
a cluster called a reef.

CORAL

CAT ISLAND

The highest peak in the country, Mt. Alvernia, is on Cat Island. It's about 210 feet above sea level.

For several hundred years, Cat Island was called "San Salvador." In 1926 it was renamed Cat Island — either for the pirate Arthur Catt, or because it was once filled with many wild cats.

SIDNEY POITIER

Sir Sidney Poitier, the award-winning actor, was raised on Cat Island. He served as the Bahamian ambassador to Japan from 1997–2007.

DEAN'S BLUE HOLE

A blue hole is a sinkhole formed millions of years ago
when limestone rock caved in and created a deep crater in the ocean.

Dean's Blue Hole is 663 feet deep.
It is one of the deepest blue holes
in the world, and is found on Long Island.

DO NOT go near a blue hole
by yourself. Only experienced
divers can swim in a blue hole.

DEAN'S BLUE HOLE
LONG ISLAND, BAHAMAS

663 FEET DEEP
NO SWIMMING

DOLPHINS

Hey look over here! I'm swimming with the dolphins!
Many species of dolphins are found in the waters
surrounding The Bahamas.

COLONEL ANDREW DEVEAUX

In 1782 the Spanish invaded the island
of New Providence. One year later, Colonel
Andrew Deveaux, a British Loyalist
from South Carolina, recaptured
Fort Montagu, Nassau, and the island.
Deveaux succeeded despite his small
force being completely outnumbered.

Deveaux plantation

Col. Andrew Deveaux

I found out that the name of the island of Eleuthera comes from the Greek word *eleutheros* which means "free." It was given this name by Captain William Sayle and a group of English Puritans who left Bermuda around 1648.

They were searching for a land to freely practice their religion, and landed at Preacher's Cave. The group became known as the Eleutheran Adventurers.

ISLAND OF ELEUTHERA

Want to know something else about Eleuthera?

Pineapples grown in Eleuthera were sold in the United States and England in the 1800s.

This fruit is a symbol of hospitality. Yum! The pineapple is so sweet! Every summer Gregory Town on Eleuthera hosts a Pineapple Festival.

PINEAPPLE FESTIVAL

PREACHER'S CAVE
1648

THE EXUMAS

The Exumas are several hundred islands and cays, including Great Exuma and Little Exuma.

NATIONAL FAMILY ISLAND REGATTA

The island of Great Exuma is home to the National Family Island Regatta. A regatta is a sailboat race. Regattas are very common in The Bahamas.

Fort Charlotte faces Nassau Harbor on the north side of the island. It's really made up of three forts.

FORT CHARLOTTE

Fort Charlotte on the eastern end was built in the late 1780s. Fort Stanley in the middle, and Fort D'Arcy on the western end, were built later.

FORT MONTAGU

The Bahamas had to defend itself against
pirates and invaders from other countries.

FORT MONTAGU
BUILT 1741

Forts were strategically placed
to protect the city of Nassau,
New Providence.

Fort Montagu is on the eastern end
of New Providence and was built in 1741.

FORT FINCASTLE

In 1793, Fort Fincastle was built on Bennet's Hill, overlooking Nassau Harbor.

There's a water tower that rises behind the fort.

FLAG

The flag of The Bahamas was raised on July 10, 1973.
This was the first day of Bahamian independence
from British rule.

The yellow represents the sun
and the sand. The blue signifies
the sea and the sky. And black
symbolizes the strength of the people.

Dr. Hervis Bain designed both
the flag and the coat of arms.

The Nassau Grouper is a favorite fish.
There are many ways to cook and serve grouper.

Because of its popularity, fishermen are only
allowed to fish for grouper from March until
the end of November. In the off-season, from
December until the end of February, the grouper
have a chance to repopulate. Conservation of
the species is very important.

GROUPER

DR. GAIL SAUNDERS

Dr. Gail Saunders is a well-known historian and author. She created The National Archives of the Bahamas and was its long-time director.

The archives is home to a number of artifacts and historical documents. It's a good place to research facts about The Bahamas.

DEPARTMENT
OF
ARCHIVES

At one time Dr. Saunders was a sprinter. She was on the first female sprint relay team to represent The Bahamas at a major international sports competition.

GRAND BAHAMA ISLAND

Atlantic Ocean

Gulf of Mexico

We are hanging out at beautiful Fortune Beach on Grand Bahama Island.

GULF STREAM

The sea water is always warm here because of the Gulf Stream. The warm water originates in the Gulf of Mexico and flows northward, through The Bahama Islands.

During the summer months, the Goombay Festival is very popular.

GOOMBAY FESTIVAL

Visitors and Bahamians alike enjoy native and popular music and food.

This is where the Governor-General hosts official functions. Government House is in the city of Nassau.

GOVERNMENT HOUSE

Hibiscus flowers are so pretty. They grow throughout The Bahamas.

HARBOUR ISLAND

I love the beautiful pink sand
that is found on Harbour Island.

FACT PRO

HARBOUR ISLAND
IS KNOWN
FOR ITS
PINK SAND

HOUSE OF ASSEMBLY

The House of Assembly is one of the Bahamian parliament's two chambers. The laws of The Bahamas are developed and debated there. The first Assembly met in 1729.

HOUSE OF ASSEMBLY

The first female speaker of the House was Rome Italia Johnson. Members of the House of Assembly represent the people of The Commonwealth of The Bahamas.

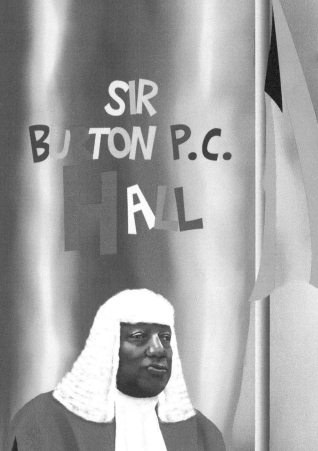

Sir Burton P.C. Hall has served
as a judge in many important
international criminal trials,
including the International
Criminal Tribunal for
the former Yugoslavia.

The International Criminal Tribunal
is part of the United Nations
and is in The Hague, Netherlands.
Sir Burton was also Chief Justice
of The Supreme Court of The Bahamas.

FACT PAD
SIR BURTON
IS A JUDGE WHO WAS
BORN IN NASSAU

INAGUA

Inagua is home to the flamingo, the national bird
of The Bahamas. Baby flamingoes have fuzzy
light gray feathers until they grow up.

Across the water are salt mounds. Inagua is home
to the second largest solar salt operation
in North America. Saltwater is evaporated by the sun,
and the salt crystals that are left behind are processed
into different types of salt.

INDEPENDENCE DAY

July 10 is Independence Day in The Bahamas. This is the day in 1973 when the country became an independent nation.

However, The Bahamas remains a member of the Commonwealth of Nations – former territories of the British Empire.

FORT FINCASTLE

JUNKANOO

Junkanoo is a festival that is celebrated twice each year: Boxing Day (December 26) and New Year's Day (January 1). It begins at midnight.

The colorful costumes are made from papier-mâché and decorated with many different types of adornments like feathers and beads.

Bands, and groups of dancers, "rush" or parade down Bay Street. The largest Junkanoo celebration takes place in Nassau, New Providence.

BAY STREET

I'm rushing down Bay Street!
Don't you love my costume?
All the bright colors,
and shaking these cowbells
as I dance, makes me happy!

KALIK!

KALIK!

"*Kalik, kalik, kalik,*"
is the sound that
the cowbells make.

What a great way to celebrate
the winter holidays!

The Lucayans were the first people to live on the Bahama Islands. They created close-knit communities and were excellent farmers, fishermen, and hunters.

The Lucayans weaved baskets, made pottery, and carved wood objects that they needed for everyday life. They were a branch of the Tainos, who lived throughout the Caribbean.

LUCAYANS

HAMMOCK

TOBACCO

ZEMI

CACIQUE

CANOE

Hammock, tobacco, zemi, canoe and *cacique,* are Lucayan/Taino words. The cacique was the leader in a Lucayan community. Zemi was a spiritual deity that was honored by the Lucayan people.

Lighthouses can be found on several islands throughout The Bahamas. They provide light which helps sailors avoid rocky and shallow waters.

This is the Elbow Reef Lighthouse. The first lighthouse was built in 1864 but had to be rebuilt in 1934.

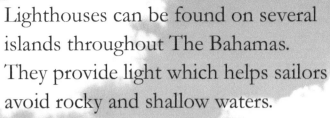

LIGNUM VITAE

The Lignum Vitae is the national tree of The Bahamas. See the purple flowers?

The wood of the tree is very hard and is used to make boat propellers.

I'm getting hungry from all our travels around the country. Let's take a break and enjoy some baked macaroni and cheese for dinner.

Yes! It's one of my favorites. You make it the same way we do, except that I notice you add chopped green sweet pepper to your macaroni. Mmmmm! Bahamian-style macaroni and cheese tastes great!

MACARONI AND CHEESE

BAHAMIAN MONEY

We'll pay for our lunch with some of this colorful Bahamian money. I love the unique shapes of the 10 cent and 15 cent pieces.

While you all enjoy your dinner, I am fishing for mine off the coast of the island of Mayaguana! I hope to catch a bonefish next. Here fishy, fishy, fishy!

MAYAGUANA

Nassau is the capital city of The Bahamas.
Nassau is located on the island of New Providence.

The City of Nassau was named
after Prince William of Orange,
who belonged to the House
of Nassau. He later became
William III, King of England.

I am from Nassau, so
I call myself a Nassuvian!

WEST SAUNDERS BEACH

MONTAGU BEACH EAST

WELCOME TO
NASSAU
1670

FACT PAD

NASSAU WAS
FOUNDED
IN 1670

NATIONAL ART GALLERY OF THE BAHAMAS

Shhhh. Be quiet, please.

I am inside the National Art Gallery of The Bahamas, where paintings by talented Bahamian artists are displayed.

ABYSSINIAN CAT

The Gallery is in an old Nassau home that's called Villa Doyle.

Olympians are athletes who participate in the Olympic Games. The Bahamas has participated in the Olympics since 1948. In 1964, Sir Durward Knowles and Mr. Cecil Cooke sailed into history as the first Bahamians to win an Olympic gold medal. The Olympic Games were held in Tokyo, Japan.

TOKYO 1964

THE BAHAMAS

JAPAN

SYDNEY 2000

RACE RESULTS   WOMEN'S 4X100 M RELAY
1ST PLACE   BAHAMAS   41.95

In 2000, the women's 4x100 meter relay race team won the gold medal at the games held in Sydney, Australia. A first for Bahamian women! The Bahamas also became the smallest nation to win an Olympic gold medal in a team event.

Women's 4 x 100	Men's 4 x 400
Savatheda Fynes	Chris Brown
Chandra Sturrup	Michael Mathieu
Pauline Davis-Thompson	Ramon Miller
Debbie Ferguson	Demetrius Pinder
Eldece Clarke-Lewis	

★ **LONDON** ★

The 2012 men's 4x400 meter relay race team captured the gold medal at the Olympic Games in London, England. They defeated the United States, which has dominated this event for over 100 years.

And they set a national record!

Athletics is the official name for track and field events.

OLYMPIANS

SIR LYNDEN OSCAR PINDLING

Sir Lynden Oscar Pindling was the first
Prime Minister of The Bahamas when
it became independent from England in 1973.

Sir Lynden was instrumental in the creation
of a government that represented the majority
of the people, not just the rights of a wealthy few.

PARADISE ISLAND

I'm over at Paradise Island.
Grandma said that this island was known
as Hog Island when she was a little girl.

There are several hotels
and resorts on Paradise Island.
You can get to this island
by crossing one of the bridges
from Nassau.

Around 1700 many pirates used The Bahamas as a base. They included Blackbeard (also known as Edward Teach), Henry Morgan, Charles Vane, Anne Bonny, Mary Read and many others.

BLACKBEARD

CHARLES VANE

HENRY MORGAN

ANNE BONNY

PIRATES

MARY READ

Piracy caused merchants and governments to lose money and property. Finally, in 1718 Governor Woodes Rogers negotiated pardons for many pirates, and others surrendered. This helped put an end to piracy in The Bahamas.

THE QUEEN'S STAIRCASE

Vanessa, what is the Queen's Staircase
and how did it get that name?

QUEEN VICTORIA

The Queen's Staircase was built
in 1794 and has 66 steps hand carved
out of solid limestone.

It was later renamed after
Queen Victoria of England,
whose reign lasted for almost
as many years as there are steps!

Can you guess on which island
the Queen's Staircase can be found?
If you said New Providence,
you are correct!

Thank you, Princess Vanessa
for the royal treatment
during our visit! You have
been an awesome tour guide!

THE ROYAL BAHAMAS POLICE FORCE BAND

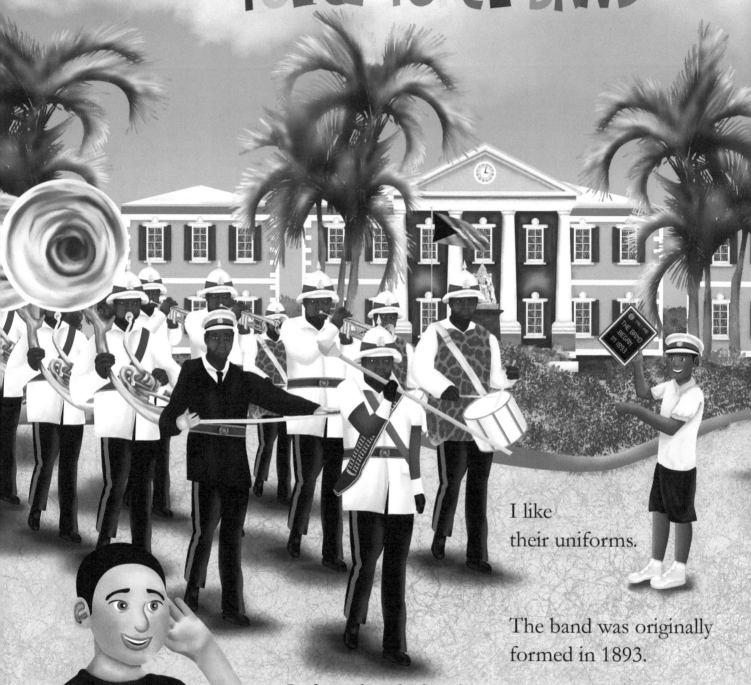

I like their uniforms.

The band was originally formed in 1893.

Is that a band I hear?
Wow, here comes
the Royal Bahamas
Police Force Band!

RAWSON SQUARE

The band performs at special occasions here in The Bahamas and has also traveled internationally.

The band is playing in Rawson Square, close to the House of Assembly, the Senate, and the Supreme Court of The Bahamas.

RAWSON   SQUARE

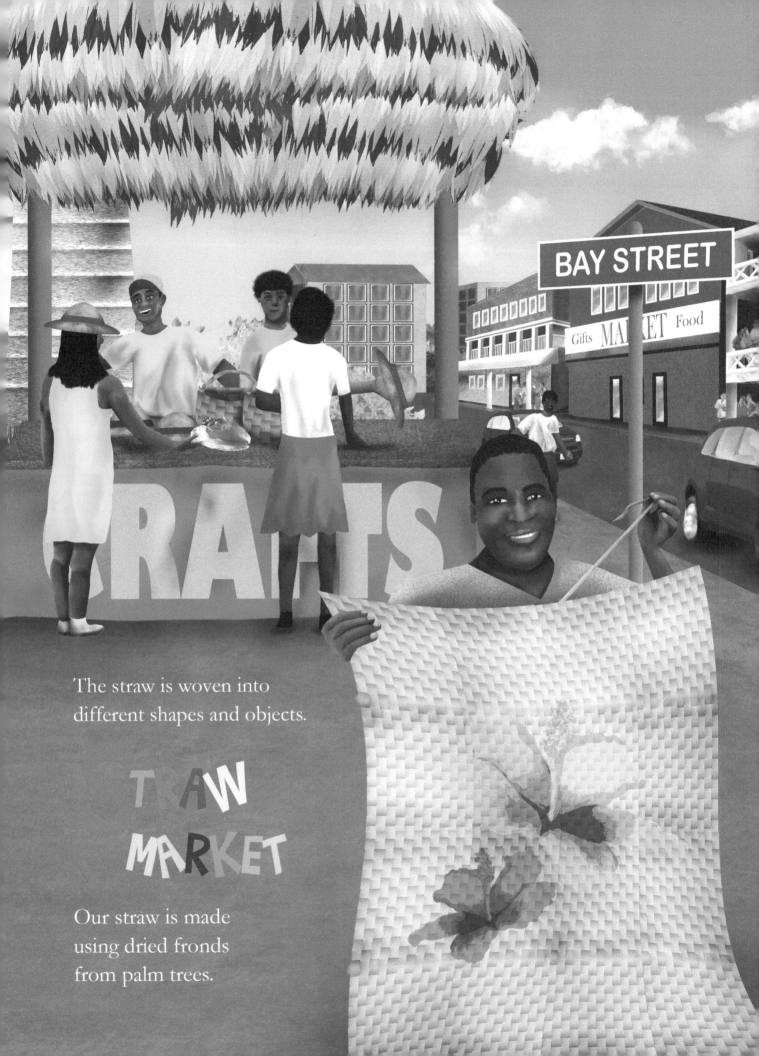

BAY STREET

Gifts MARKET Food

CRAFTS

The straw is woven into
different shapes and objects.

STRAW
MARKET

Our straw is made
using dried fronds
from palm trees.

I found a sand dollar here at the beach.
Sand dollars are related to sea urchins and starfish.

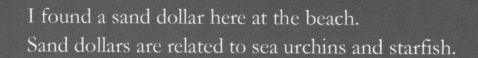

SAND
DOLLAR

Live sand dollars
are a purple color.

This white, flat disk is really
the sand dollar's skeleton!

STARFISH

Look! I found a starfish.

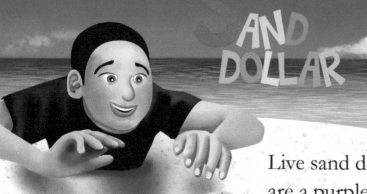

These colorful animals aren't
actually fish because they don't
have fins, tails, or gills!
Instead they are echinoderms
and use tiny feet to move.

Scientists prefer to call them sea stars.

We're down here on the island of San Salvador. It was originally inhabited by the Lucayan/Taino people.

San Salvador

San Salvador is the island where the Italian explorer Christopher Columbus landed on October 12, 1492. The cross on the beach represents where he and his sailors may have made landfall.

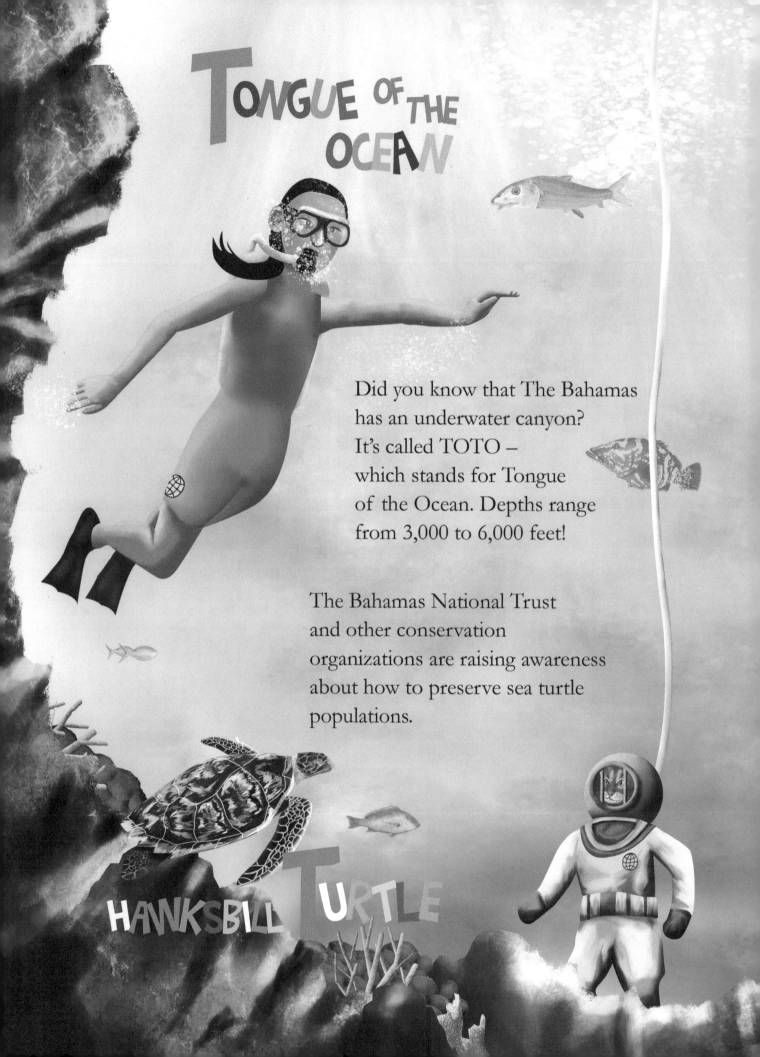

TONGUE OF THE OCEAN

Did you know that The Bahamas
has an underwater canyon?
It's called TOTO –
which stands for Tongue
of the Ocean. Depths range
from 3,000 to 6,000 feet!

The Bahamas National Trust
and other conservation
organizations are raising awareness
about how to preserve sea turtle
populations.

HAWKSBILL TURTLE

GREEN TURTLE

Turtles are large, but they are graceful swimmers.

Four species of turtles live in The Bahamas: the hawksbill, the loggerhead, the leatherback, and the green turtle. Each of these species of turtle is endangered.

Tongue of the Ocean

LEATHERBACK TURTLE

LOGGERHEAD TURTLE

UNION CREEK RESERVE

The beautiful Union Creek Reserve is part
of the Bahamas National Trust,
which manages the national parks of The Bahamas.

This nature preserve is on the island
of Great Inagua.

UNION CREEK
RESERVE

"Forward, Upward, Onward, Together" is the national motto found on the Coat of Arms of The Bahamas.

As a nation, The Bahamas continues to move forward into the future. The goal is to reach upward and onward to new opportunities, together as a united people.

UPWARD

"FORWARD, UPWARD, ONWARD,

TOGETHER."

E.P. ROBERTS PRIMARY SCHOOL

Wow, I love the uniforms that the policemen and policewomen wear here. I especially like their hats!

Guess what?

I wear a uniform to school too. All school age youth wear uniforms to school. I get dressed so quickly in the morning because I do not have to decide what to wear.

UNIFORMS

VERSAILLES GARDEN

The Versailles Gardens were created by a wealthy businessman on Paradise Island.

The Cloisters in the gardens was originally built in the 14th century in France. It was brought to The Bahamas piece by piece!

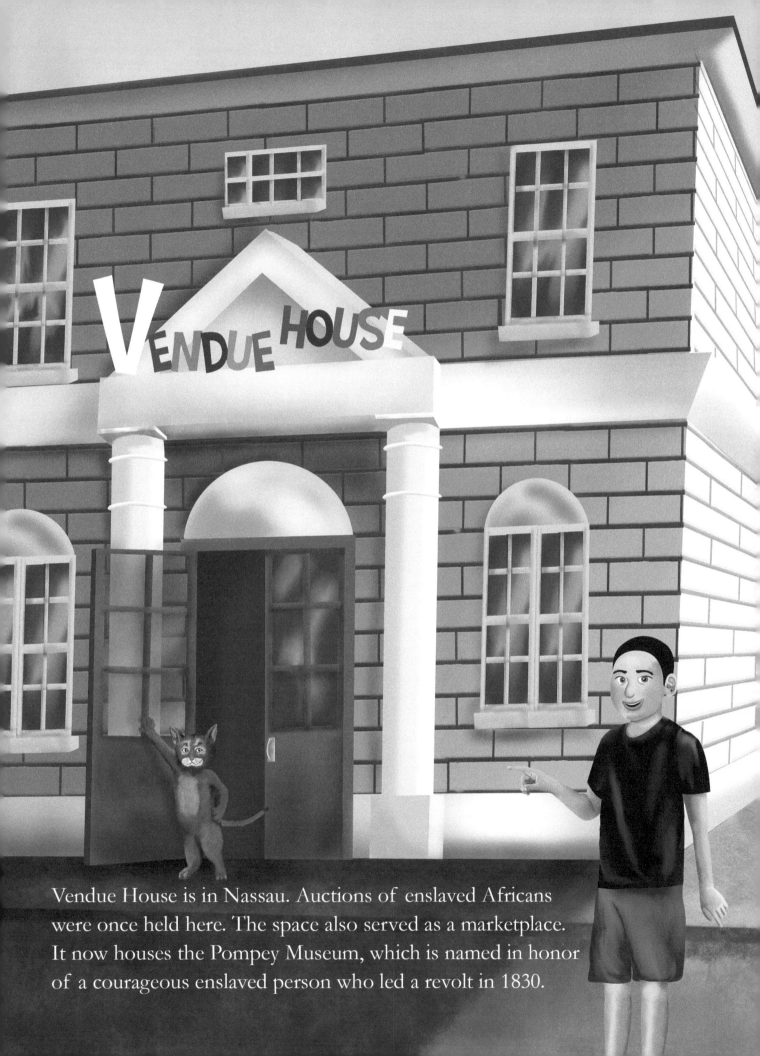

Vendue House is in Nassau. Auctions of enslaved Africans were once held here. The space also served as a marketplace. It now houses the Pompey Museum, which is named in honor of a courageous enslaved person who led a revolt in 1830.

WAHOO

Wahoo! Boy, these fish are fast swimmers.

There are several wahoo fishing tournaments that take place in The Bahamas.

Wahoo can travel up to 60 miles per hour and swim either by themselves or in small groups – which are called schools.

WAHOO
FISHING TOURNAMENT

WATER TOWER

Many years ago, the water tower was used to control water pressure throughout homes on the island of New Providence. It has 216 steps and is one of the tallest structures in Nassau.

WALKER'S CAY

Walker's Cay is the island that is found at the northern end of the Bahamian archipelago. It is part of The Abacos.

WALKER'S CAY

Ahoy there! Did you know that the first flag
of The Bahamas had an "X" on it?"

The coat of arms on the flag
says *Expulsis Piratus.*
Restitua Commercia.
That means, "Pirates, out.
Commerce restored."

Good research, everyone!

I'm sure it was hard to find
an item for the letter "X"
for our alphabet adventure.
But you did it!!

S.S. EVANGELINE

YELLOW ELDER

Evan, did you know that the yellow elder is the national flower of The Bahamas?

Yes, I did.
The flowers are bright yellow and shaped like trumpets.

YELLOWTAIL SNAPPER

I went diving and saw a school
of yellowtail snapper.
They are fast swimmers.

Already up to letter "Y"?
You all are fast fact finders!

BOA
CONSTRICTOR

The male peacock
is able to spread his
feathers like a fan.

GOLD
MACAW

LEMUR

PEACOCK

FLAMINGOS

You all did a great job
exploring the islands
of The Bahamas.

YELLOW-CROWNED
NIGHT-HERON

Thanks, everyone.
We learned facts about the culture,
history, and people from A to Z.
Now I can finish my report about The Bahamas!

I can't wait
until our next voyage!

WELCOME TO
THE BAHAMAS

See you all again soon.
Travel safely!

The Bahamas from A to Z

Now that our adventure is over, let's review some of the amazing things that we saw along the way. Can you look back and find them? They might not be on the page you expect!

A Archipelago

B Sir Milo Butler

B Bonefish

C Conch Shell

D Dean's Blue Hole

D Dolphin

E Edward Teach

F Flag

F Flamingo

G Nassau Grouper

G Goombay Festival Musician

H House of Assembly

H Hibiscus

I Ixora

I Iguana

J Junkanoo Drummer

K Kalik! Kalik! Cowbell

L — Lucayan — Elbow Reef Lighthouse

M — Macaroni and Cheese — Marlin

N — National Art Gallery Statue — ABYSSINIAN CAT

O — Olympian — BAH

P — Bahama Parrot — Pineapple

Q — Queen Victoria

R — Royal Bahamas Police Force Band — Mary Read

S — Starfish — Dr. Gail Saunders

T — Green Turtle

U — Student in School Uniform

V — Versailles Garden Statue

W — Water Tower — Wahoo

X — eXpulsis Piratus — EXPULSIS PIRATIS COMMERCIA RESTITUTA BAHAMAS

Y — Yellow Elder — Yellowtail Snapper

Z — Zemi

About the Author

Veronica McFall has over 25 years of combined professional experience in K-12 and higher education, as well as educational not-for-profits.

A graduate of Colgate University, Veronica attended Teachers College, Columbia University as a Mellon Fellow, and received an MA in Bilingual/Bicultural Education, and an M.Ed. in Curriculum and Instruction.

Veronica has a passion for the limitless opportunity education provides. *A Visit to The Bahamas from A to Z* is her first book. It is also the inaugural title in a series that aims to encourage youth travel and cross-cultural understanding.

Veronica McFall lives in New Jersey with her husband. They have three children who are on their own voyage into adulthood.

About the Illustrator

A Visit to the Bahamas from A to Z is illustrator RJ Jenkins' first book for children. A graduate of Bates College, RJ is a visual arts teacher and a basketball, track and cross country coach at a college preparatory school in Maine. RJ has a passion for helping young people realize their creative talents. During his many years as an educator, RJ has taught a wide range of art, design, and film production courses, and has also worked on a number of design and marketing projects for the school.

RJ enjoys spending time with his wife and two children, being active in the outdoors of Maine, watching movies, drawing and painting, and gathering with his close-knit family.

Do you want to know how we checked all of the facts in the book? Visit **knowledgeiscapital.com** to find out.

KNOWLEDGE is CAPITAL
PUBLISHING & EDUCATIONAL PROGRAMS

CPSIA information can be obtained
at www.ICGtesting.com
Printed in the USA
LVHW070949261222
735896LV00021B/112